D0987760

KNOW HOW KNOW WHY

INCREDIBLE INSECTS

Written by Lucy Bater

Illustrations by John Butler

TOP THAT

Licensed exclusively to Top That Publishing Ltd
Tide Mill Way, Woodbridge, Suffolk, IP12 1AP, UK
www.topthatpublishing.com
Copyright © 2013 Tide Mill Media
All rights reserved
0 2 4 6 8 9 7 5 3 1
Printed and bound in China

FLYING COLOURS

Fossils show that insects have lived on Earth for at least 320 million years – even before there were dinosaurs! These amazing creatures come in all sorts of shapes and sizes and can be found all over our planet, from jungles and deserts to houses and gardens. But what exactly is an insect?

What is an insect ?

An insect's body is made of three essential parts – the head, thorax and abdomen. Unlike humans, insects have exoskeletons – skeletons on the outside of their bodies. This protects them from harm and ensures that water stays inside, preventing their bodies from drying out. Many insects have wings, and the majority have antennae close to the head. Insects rank among some of the most successful animals in the world. With millions of species, they can live in almost any habitat. Insects are known as arthropods, animals which lack a backbone.

What are arachnids ?

Arachnids have eight (sometimes ten) legs and are made of two distinct body parts – the abdomen and the cephalothorax (a combination of the head and thorax). They have a pair of fang-like mouthparts and a pair of leg-like structures that come in useful for holding food. Scorpions, mites, ticks, crane flys (daddy long-legs) and spiders are all part of the arachnid family.

FACT BYTES

Stick insects are the longest insects in the world.

African stick insects can be as long as 40 cm (16 in.).

Do insects grow

An insect's hard exoskeleton cannot grow, which makes it difficult for the insect to get any bigger. Insects grow by breaking out of and shedding their skin. When this has happened, they have to grow before their new skin hardens. This process is called 'moulting'. Once they become adults, insects don't get any bigger.

How long do insects live ?

Different insects have different lifespans. Mayflies live for less than a day; some butterflies live for several days. Many insects are seasonal and live for a year, mating, laying eggs and then dying. However, there are some exceptions. A queen termite, for example, can live for up to fifty years!

Do insects hibernate ?

Being cold-blooded, insects tend to prefer warmer climates and have adapted in a number of ways to cope with the cold. In the winter, some insects hibernate through a process called diapause, which makes them stop moving, preserving energy. Some adult insects can stop the water in their bodies from freezing by producing a chemical called glycerol that acts like anti-freeze. Honeybees stay in clusters in their hives and use their vibrating wing muscles to raise the temperature to keep each other warm when it's cold!

Honeybees stay in clusters to keep warm.

FLYING COLORS

WHAT'S BUGGING YOU?

Bedbugs, assassin bugs, flat bugs, seed bugs, red bugs, stink bugs, plant bugs ... there are around 80,000 different types of bug that make up the group of insects known as Hemiptera. All the insects in this group have something in common – sucking mouthparts.

Do bed bugs really bite

A bed bug

Night night, sleep tight, don't let the bedbugs bite ... The bad news is that, yes, bedbugs really do bite! They commonly hide in mattresses and the cracks in bed frames during the day, but crawl out at night to feast on snoozing humans. The good news is that bedbugs don't transmit diseases and, apart from leaving you with a few itchy patches, if they bite you won't feel a thing!

What makes a stink bug stink

A stink bug

Put yourself in a stink bug's shoes ... there's a big bird about to pounce on you and gobble you up, and in a matter of moments you're going to be history – so what would you do? You'd need to unleash a hidden defence so you can live to see another day. That's exactly what a stink bug does. Its hidden defence is its pong – phew. One whiff of this smelly perfume and predators think twice!

How did the assassin bug get its name

An assassin bug

Lurking in the undergrowth, waiting to ambush its prey, the assassin bug lies in wait, preparing to attack. This bug is a killer (hence its name), and eats other insects by stabbing them with its proboscis and then injecting them with a lethal dose of saliva. This toxic saliva turns the inside of the victim's body into liquid, and the assassin bug sucks up what it probably considers to be a delicious meal. If an assassin bug can't find a suitable insect to eat, it will quite happily eat a fellow assassin bug rather than go hungry!

How and what do bugs eat

Bugs feed through a long, hollow tube called a proboscis. They pierce their food and then suck up the juices. Some bugs suck up plant juices, called sap, but there are other more sinister bugs in existence that like to suck blood and body fluids. These bugs often have legs covered in tiny hairs, which help them to hold on to their victims while they feed.

Scientists use electronic microscopes to magnify specimens, such as this bedbug, thousands of times.

Are bugs able to live underwater as well as on land

Many bugs have adapted to life in or around water. Water boatmen swim upside down, using two long legs like oars, which make them look like tiny rowing boats. They paddle through the water, chasing and catching tadpoles and small fish to eat. Giant water bugs are so large that they can catch and eat frogs and bigger fish. Water measurers can be found at the edges of ponds. They 'skate' across the water's surface, stabbing at mosquito larvae with their piercing mouthparts.

A water boatman

Do bugs use disguise

Many bugs use disguise to protect themselves from predators, and it's easy to see how the thorn bug got its name – after all, no predator would like to eat a sharp thorn. Thorn bugs like to suck sap, so tend to gather in groups on the stems of plants, which makes them look even more prickly!

FACT BYTES

Ambush bugs, which mainly live in the tropical Americas and Asia, are stealthy insects, as they rely on camouflage to disguise them as they wait to catch their prey.

BEETLE MANIA

With around 400,000 different kinds, beetles form the largest group of insects, known as Coleoptera. The word 'Coleoptera' means 'sheathed wing', and you'll see that most beetles' flight wings are protected by a hardened shield.

Which beetle is also known as a cocktail **?**

When threatened, the devil's coach-horse beetle arches its tail and opens its pincer-like jaws, rather like a scorpion. (Its arched tail means it is also known as a 'cock-tail'.) If this action doesn't put off predators, the beetle squirts a stinking liquid from two glands at its rear.

The devil's coach-horse beetle has no sting in its tail, but squirts a foul-smelling liquid and gives a nasty bite.

What is a blister beetle **?**

Some beetles secrete toxic chemicals when threatened. If the poisonous chemical secreted by the blister beetle touches human skin, it causes painful blisters and can even be fatal if swallowed. This chemical, called cantharidin, is secreted by the male beetle and given to the

A blister beetle

female, who covers her eggs with it to protect them from predators. Blister beetles are often brightly coloured, which acts as a further warning to predators to stay away – these beetles are bad to eat!

Where do baby dung beetles live **?**

All that hard work cleaning up the earth and burying dung balls means that female scarab (or dung) beetles are able to lay their eggs in privacy underground in the dung!
As the worm babies hatch they dig into, and live happily inside, the dung ball, before coming up for air as adult dung beetles.

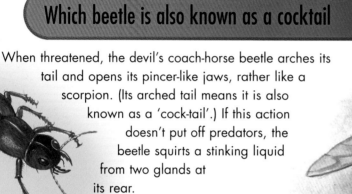
Stag beetles.

Which beetle looks like a deer

If you've ever seen a male stag beetle flying low on summer evenings you'll know the answer. This mighty beetle, one of the biggest in Europe, can be as big as 7 cm (3in.) and has magnificent antler-like jaws. Like deer, these antlers come in very handy when wrestling with another male for the best breeding site.

Which are the largest and smallest beetles

Some large, tropical beetles can grow to be as big as a human hand, whereas the smallest types can barely be seen. The heaviest beetle is the adult goliath beetle, which can measure up to 15 cm (6 in.) in length and weigh up to 100 g (4 oz) – this heavyweight is bigger than your fist! Although thinner, some stick insects are over 30 cm (12 in.) in length! Feather-winged beetles, on the other hand, are the smallest beetles in the world. They can barely be seen by the human eye and look like specks of dust.

The goliath beetle is a real heavyweight.

Were dung beetles worshipped

The ancient Egyptians were fascinated by a type of dung beetle known as the scarab. As scarab beetles busily rolled balls of dung along the ground, their bright, almost metallic colouring reminded the Egyptians of the sun crossing Earth. The scarab symbol was soon used as a good luck charm to ward off evil and symbolise immortality. Keep a look out in history books to see pictures of the scarab on ancient Egyptian tombs and jewellery.

FACT BYTES

The acteon beetle from South America can grow to be a chunky 9 cm (3½ in.) long, 5cm (2 in.) wide and 4 cm (1½ in.) thick!

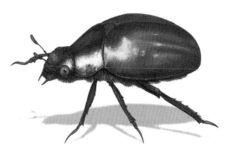

A scarab or "dung" beetle

BEETLE MANIA

EYE SPY DRAGONFLY

Dragonflies are one of the oldest types of insect. They first appeared in the Carboniferous period, around 320 million years ago and way before dinosaurs walked on Earth. These ancient insects were much larger than modern-day dragonflies, and some fossilised examples have been found with wingspans of close to a metre!

Where did the dragonfly get its name ?

A dragonfly dentist would soon be able to tell you! Dragonflies belong to the family Odonata, which means 'toothed jaw'. Imagine how scary these powerful jaws must look to an unsuspecting prey insect. In the Middle Ages, flies had a bad name. The term dragonfly probably reflects this negative attitude towards flies. You may also hear the dragonfly being referred to by one of these other names, none of which are very flattering: adder bolt, snake doctor, mosquito hawk, devil's riding horse, horse stinger and devil's darning needle.

Why do dragonflies live by water ?

Dragonflies are often seen near water because this is where the female lays her eggs. When the eggs hatch, the larvae (called nymphs) live beneath the water, breathing through gills and feeding on tadpoles and small fish. Dragonflies stay in this larval state for up to five years. When they are ready to become adults, they climb up a reed or piece of plant matter, where their old larval skin spilts overnight and a beautiful dragonfly emerges in the warmth of the morning sun.

Can they see you coming ?

Like many insects, a dragonfly's eyes take up most of its head, giving it a 360-degree field of vision. Each human eye has just one lens, but a dragonfly has many thousands of lenses in each eye (called compound eyes). This means it can see in front, above, below and behind – perfect for detecting the slightest movement, whether to catch prey or escape from danger.

Why is a dragonfly also called a mosquito hawk

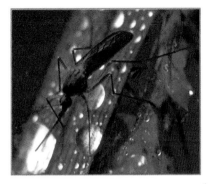

Adult dragonflies catch their prey in flight. A typical dragonfly meal consists of any of the following ingredients – mosquitoes, midges, gnats, wasps and flies. Thanks to its liking for the dreaded mosquito, humans are a big fan of dragonflies, so if you're near a riverbank on a hot summer's day, let's hope the dragonflies are there hunting mosquitoes.

Is a dragonfly a fly

While it's true that both dragonflies and flies are insects, flies have just two wings, whereas dragonfiles have four. So, a dragonfly is not a type of fly. As a general rule, most insects have four wings; flies are the exception.

Why does a dragonfly have hairy legs

A dragonfly's legs are covered in short bristles. When the dragonfly is out hunting for a tasty snack, its hairy legs form an oval-shaped basket that scoop its prey right out of the air - just like a shopping basket!

FACT BYTES

One of the largest dragonflies, *Megaloprepus coerulatus*, has a wingspan of up to 19 cm (7 ½ in.).

How fast can a dragonfly actually fly

Dragonflies can beat each pair of wings independently: their front wings go down while the back ones come up. This makes all dragonflies excellent fliers. They can loop-the-loop, hover and even fly backwards! These amazing wings enable most large dragonflies to reach speeds of about 30 kph (18 mph), but the Australian dragonfly, Austrophlebia costalis, beats them all. It has been recorded at an incredible 58 kph (36 mph)!

GIVE IT UP FOR GRASSHOPPERS

Grasshoppers belong to the insect family called Orthoptera. The word 'Orthoptera' comes from the Greek words 'orthos' meaning 'straight' and 'ptera' meaning 'wing'. As well as grasshoppers, this family of 20,000 different species includes locusts, crickets, ground hoppers and katydids.

Where did the wart-biter get its name ❓

There is one type of cricket with extremely powerful jaws known as a wart-biter, and, guess what – it was once used to bite warts off human skin.

The wart-biter cricket was once used to bite off skin.

How do they communicate ❓

Listen carefully as you pass patches of tall grass in the summer and you might be lucky enough to hear crickets and grasshoppers chirping. This sound, known as 'stridulation', is not made by a voice, but by a row of bumps on the insect's legs or wings. The insect rubs its hind legs against its forewings or, in some cases, rubs its wings together to make the noise. Each species has a different arrangement of bumps, so the sounds they make are unique. Next time you hear a grasshopper chirp, take it as a sign that love is in the air! It's the males that 'sing' to woo the females and to warn off other males.

A pair of mating crickets

How do grasshoppers hear ?

Grasshoppers and crickets don't have ears on their heads, but they can still hear and feel vibrations. A grasshopper's ears (called tympanum) are on the sides of its body, whereas a cricket's ears can be seen as a swelling just below each knee on its front legs.

What is a plague of locusts ?

Locusts usually live alone … until it rains. Rain provides locusts with the perfect conditions to reproduce, and they go into a breeding frenzy, producing millions – and sometimes billions – of offspring. The close contact between these insects can cause them to become what is known as gregarious. They appear different to their parents, changing colour from the usual green to multicoloured pink, black and yellow, and form enormous groups called swarms.

Locusts can cause serious damage to farmers' crops.

FACT BYTES

Since Biblical times, locusts and grasshoppers have provided tasty snacks for humans. John the Baptist was said to have lived on locusts and honey, and today these insects, which contain fifty per cent protein, still feature as a standard ingredient in Middle Eastern and Chinese cuisine. Simply remove the wings, the small legs and the head, season and serve!

FLUTTERBY BUTTERFLY

Butterflies and moths are both part of the Lepidoptera group – 'lepido' meaning 'scale' and 'ptera' meaning 'wing'. This is the second-largest group of insects, with over 15,000 species of butterfly and 150,000 species of moth.

Can butterflies resist injury ?

As a rule, no – but the monarch butterfly has evolved a kind of leathery skin. Birds often peck at butterflies on their thorax which usually kills them, but the monarch's tougher skin can withstand the bird's pecking. The bird, expecting an easy meal, becomes confused and, in the confusion, the monarch flies away unharmed. An ordinary butterfly would be pecked to pieces and gobbled up, but the monarch survives.

What's the difference between butterflies and moths ?

Butterflies and moths can be tricky to tell apart, but take a closer look and you'll soon be able to spot the differences. Both have four wings, which are covered in tiny coloured scales that look like dust. Butterflies are usually brightly coloured, and show off their beautiful wings during the day. When they stop to rest, they close their wings, which have a duller pattern on the underside. Butterflies have slim, smooth bodies, with a bulge at the end of each antenna, known as feelers. Moths, on the other hand, are nocturnal (they fly at night), and their wings are often muted brown, grey, white or black in colour. This colouring keeps them camouflaged during the day, when they rest with their wings open. Moths are usually fat and furry, and they have feathery, comb-like antennae, which scientists believe helps them to smell and sense movement.

How does a butterfly taste its food ?

If you've watched a butterfly resting on a leaf, consider that you might have interrupted its lunch! Butterflies taste through their feet. The female also does this to check whether a plant is the right variety to lay her eggs on.

FACT BYTES

Most adult butterflies drink nectar from flowers through their proboscis – a feeding tube that they can unroll and use like a straw to suck up this sweet-tasting liquid.

What's the biggest butterfly

Well, for a start she's female and she's named after a queen … the Queen Alexandra birdwing. This rare and poisonous beauty has a wingspan of up to 28 cm (11 in.), with pale markings on a dark chocolate-brown background and a bright yellow abdomen. Both the males and the females fly high in the rainforest canopy of Papua New Guinea.

The Queen Alexandra birdwing

Which moth sounds like a bird

If you're lucky enough to come across the hummingbird hawk moth, you could be forgiven for thinking it's a bird – especially as, to confuse you further, it flies during the daytime! This expert hoverer darts from flower to flower, beating its wings as it does so until you can hear it hum. It has a wingspan of 5.8 cm (2in.) and is often mistaken for a hummingbird.

A hummingbird hawk moth

What's the largest moth

The atlas moth is a truly impressive sight and has the largest wing area of any moth in the world. It lives in the jungles of Malaysia, and uses the large white 'eye spots' on its beautiful ruby-coloured wings to warn off predators. Despite its defence camouflage, the atlas moth has a sad tale to tell. While the atlas caterpillar munches as much as it can in order to develop into this mammoth moth, the atlas moth itself has no stomach. This means that it cannot take in food, and so lives for only around a day.

An atlas moth

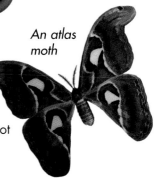

FLUTTERBY BUTTERFLY

BUSY BODIES

There are over 19,000 known species of bee and a similar number of wasp – but these are only the ones we know about! Both bees and wasps are a gardener's friend, as bees pollinate flowers and wasps like to eat common garden pests, such as caterpillars and aphids.

Why do wasps like picnics ?

Wasps love sugary foods, so a picnic for you is a picnic for them too! Throughout the summer they are busy feeding their young, so don't tend to bother people, but by the end of the season they are at their most annoying as they search for their favourite sugary snacks (such as ice creams, fizzy drinks and fruit). If you prepare a separate picnic for the wasps – perhaps a plate of sweet, sticky jam or a bottle of cola – and put it at a safe distance, they can join in without upsetting your fun. Remember, though, always look out for them before you sit down, put your hands down or take a bite of your picnic lunch.

How do bees make honey ?

Bees produce honey from a sugary liquid called nectar. They suck the nectar from flowers and store it in a special honey stomach, which is in addition to their regular stomach. Filling this stomach takes between 100–1,500 visits to flowers and, when full, can weigh almost as much as the bee does! On returning to the hive, the nectar is passed to worker bees, who digest it and regurgitate it as raw honey. It is then spread through honeycomb and fanned dry by the bees' wings until it becomes thick and gooey. The honey is stored for the bees to eat throughout the year.

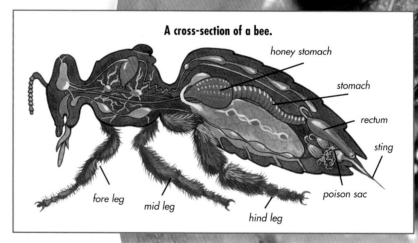

A cross-section of a bee.

honey stomach

stomach

rectum

sting

poison sac

fore leg

mid leg

hind leg

What is the difference between bees and wasps

You may think that all bees and wasps are just buzzing, stinging, yellow-and-black insects, but there are ways to tell them apart. Bees have short hairs all over their bodies – even their eyes – which makes them look soft and fuzzy. Bumble bees are larger and rounder than honey bees, but they are still hairy. Bees feed on nectar and pollen, and can often be seen carrying pollen back to their hives in little 'baskets' on their hind legs. Wasps, on the other hand, have a thin 'waist' and a smooth, shiny body. Their yellow-and-black markings are much sharper and brighter than bees'. Wasps chew up wood to make a nest of paper, and instead of collecting nectar, they prey on other insects. Many bees and wasps are social insects, which means they live and work together as a colony. A colony may comprise thousands of insects, but is always centred on a queen bee or wasp, who is larger than the others and the only one to lay eggs.

Why do bees and wasps sting

The yellow and black colours of bees and wasps act as a warning to say that these insects sting! While a sting can be painful and, in a few people, cause a serious allergic reaction, bees and wasps usually attack only when they feel threatened. A bee can sting only once. This is because a little hook on the end of its stinger catches in whatever it decides to sting, causing its abdomen to tear as it flies away. The bee dies as a result. Wasps, on the other hand, can sting many times.

How can I avoid being stung

FACT BYTES

The tarantula hawk wasp is also the biggest wasp in the world with a wingspan of about 12 cm (5in.).

Not every bee or wasp is out to sting you. Remember, they usually attack only when they feel threatened, and this might be because you are standing too close to their nest (you may not even realise it). If a wasp or bee comes closer to you than you'd like, just walk away calmly. If you wave your arms about and start to panic, you'll probably just convince it that you really are a threat.

ANT-TASTIC

Ants and termites are known as 'social' insects because they live in groups. The group could be as few as twenty or as large as many thousands and is called a colony. Did you know that there are more termites on Earth than human beings?

How is a colony of ants made up

A colony is made up of lots of small rooms, or chambers, which are joined together by a network of tunnels. The colony is built and looked after by thousands of worker ants. Worker ants are also known as 'neuter' ants, which means that they can't breed. As well as maintaining the colony, they gather food, look after the young ants, defend the colony and look after the queen – the largest ant and the only one to lay eggs in the colony. Most of the eggs that the queen lays develop into worker ants, but certain 'special' eggs develop into ants of separate sexes, both male and female. Unlike their neuter family members, these males and females have wings, so set off to mate on what is known as their 'nuptial flight'. Once mated, each female becomes the queen of a new colony.

What do ants eat

Ants eat anything from small invertebrates and the bodies of dead animals to fruit, seeds and fungus. Ants have very strong mouthparts, called mandibles, so can easily cut up pieces of food. Some ants like honeydew – the sweet liquid made by tiny green insects called aphids. The ants protect groups of aphids and keep them like herds of cows to 'milk' for honeydew.

An ant's powerful mandibles can cut up its food.

Which termites make the tallest nest

The African termite takes the prize! Starting underground, its nest can measure up to 12.8 m (42ft) high, emerging above the earth with umbrella-shaped layers. That's the equivalent of seven tall people standing on top of one another.

A cross-section of a termite nest

How do ants communicate

Ants have two ways of communicating in order to pass on messages about the nest, their food or their enemies. They do this by creating special chemicals called pheromones that other ants can smell. If this doesn't work, they take a more direct approach and use their antennae to tap their message on to another ant!

What does a queen ant do

The queen ant's sole responsibility is to lay eggs, making sure that the colony continues to grow. This means that all the other ants in the colony must look after her, clean her, protect her and feed her. What a great life for the queen!

Where does the honeypot ant get its name

If you'd ever seen one you'd know why! This amazing ant lives in semi-desert regions and during the rainy season, it's fed with water and nectar until its abdomen swells up. Then, when the dry season starts and there's not much food around, it can regurgitate the food and be a useful walking larder to the other hungry ants. Dig in!

A honey pot ant.

ANT-TASTIC

FACT BYTES

Termites not only like to eat wood, but enjoy chewing on books, carpets, furniture, window frames and flooring.

In some countries, termite damage in a house is a bigger threat than tornado, fire, lightning or even a hurricane!

Worker ants with the queen

EAT UP

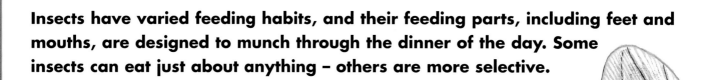

Insects have varied feeding habits, and their feeding parts, including feet and mouths, are designed to munch through the dinner of the day. Some insects can eat just about anything – others are more selective.

What do insects eat ?

Insects enjoy a varied menu and will eat just about anything, depending on the species. An insect supper includes plants, nectar, other insects, blood, fruit, seeds and human food. Sometimes an insect's mouthparts are designed to suit a certain purpose. A weevil, for example, has tiny jaws at the end of a curved snout. It bites (or drills) tiny holes in plants.

A weevil

How does a praying mantis eat its prey ?

The praying mantis looks suspiciously leaf-like. Its green colour enables it to stalk its prey before grabbing it with its spiky front legs. It then uses its mighty jaws to slice through the victim's body.

A praying mantis

How do mosquitoes spread disease ?

Mosquitoes drink blood and any viruses that are contained within it. When the mosquito feasts on a new victim, it can pass on diseases, such as malaria. The mosquito is responsible for more human deaths in Africa than any other creature.

FACT BYTES

'Maggot Therapy' is a medical technique that uses hungry maggots to clean wounds with dead or rotten flesh. It has a long history and is still used up to the present day.

Which beetle has the most disgusting feeding habit

Glossy, dark-coloured carrion beetles love to munch on the decomposing flesh of dead animals. Sometimes they hide beneath it; at other times you may see them wandering around the insides of the rotting body. However, these beetles cannot live on decomposing flesh alone and die if they do not have a healthy supply of maggots to keep them going.

A carrion beetle

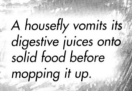

A housefly vomits its digestive juices onto solid food before mopping it up.

What are parasites

A parasite is any animal that lives off another, different animal without giving anything in return. The itch mite is a good example of this and can live off humans who do not wear sufficient protective clothing. The mite burrows underneath the skin and lays eggs, which emerge as larvae two or three days later. All this activity under the skin can be itchy, with scratching making it worse, leading to infection.

Why are house flies sick

To find out whether something is good to eat, a housefly tastes it with its feet, which are thought to be ten million times more sensitive to sugar than the human tongue. A housefly can't bite, so if it wants to eat solid food it has to spread its digestive juices over it – rather like vomiting! The food turns soft, and the fly can then dab at it with its sponge-like mouthparts.

What does an ant use mandibles for

Ants have jaws specifically designed to chop up food and these are known as mandibles. The ant uses these mandibles to bite and cut up its food, for excavation, to build nests and as a weapon.

LEGGY, LEGGY, LEGGY!

You've seen creepy-crawlies scuttle and crawl along floors and up walls, but have you ever stopped to wonder just how amazing their legs are? Evolution has allowed some insects to use their legs in incrediable ways.

Which insect is the best jumper

The hind legs of the flea are very strong, making them one of the best animal jumpers of all in comparison to their body size. There are thought to be over 2,000 species of flea in the world, but cat and dog fleas are two of the most common to be found in people's homes. These blood-sucking insects use their powerful hind legs to jump from one host (or meal) to another. Fleas can jump as high as 30 cm (12 in.), accelerating as fast as a space rocket!

How many legs does a millipede have

A centipede

The word 'millipede' literally means 'a thousand legs'. Plant-eating millipedes do not, in fact, have that many legs; the leggiest of all only has 710 legs. A millipede's legs move rhythmically beneath it, and are hidden under its body. Centipedes are often confused with millipedes. They have fewer, more visible legs and are voracious predators!

Do insects use their legs in self-defence

Native Americans once called the Jerusalem cricket 'Woh-tzi Neh,' which means 'old bald-headed man'. At 5 cm (2 in.) in length it may look fearsome, it doesn't sting and isn't poisonous – so how does it protect itself from harm? Instead of using its strong hind legs to jump away from danger like other crickets might, they help it perform a disappearing act! When threatened, it uses the spikes on its powerful hind legs to dig a hole in the soil or sand and disappears to safety underground.

How do water beetles escape predators

One type of water beetle, the camphor beetle, uses its legs to ski on the water's surface. To escape from predators, it shoots a chemical from its back legs that reduces the water surface tension. This means that the tension on its front legs pulls it forwards. It zooms out of trouble on its front feet, which are held out like skis, and steers itself by flexing its abdomen. This tiny beetle is the size of a rice grain, but can travel nearly a metre per second. Another water beetle, the whirligig, dives into water to avoid predators, breathing from a bubble of air trapped in its rear end.

The Jerusalem cricket uses its powerful hind legs to dig into the ground.

How does a locust jump

A locust ready to lift off is an impressive sight. First, it keeps its hind legs folded ready to jump. Then the leg muscles straighten out, launching the insect into the air. High in the air, the locust uses its wings to fly forwards, before spreading its legs wide to ensure a safe landing.

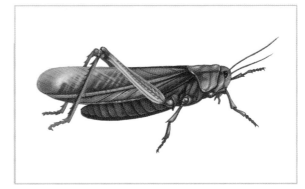

A locust ready to jump

A locust using its wings to fly

A locust beginning to land

FACT BYTES

Giant crane flies (daddy-long-legs) have breakaway legs that enable them to fly off if caught. The predator is left with a spindly leg, and the crane fly can survive with five of its six legs.

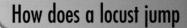

LEGGY, LEGGY, LEGGY!

STAYING ALIVE

It's a jungle out there – particularly for insects struggling to survive without being eaten by predators! Insects have developed cunning means of self-defence, and some even re-grow injured legs or antennae.

Which beetle is the most scary ?

Stay away from a bombardier beetle! As is common in the natural world, their red colouring could be a warning signal. *Danger! Stay away!* When this beetle is angry or provoked, it fires a mixture of chemicals from special glands situated in its rear end. One species fires the chemicals as a constant jet (like a hose), and other types release their spray at intervals. A complicated system of chemical reactions take place inside the body of the beetle, creating such a high pressure that boiling point is reached.

What is a 'toe biter' ?

The giant water bug has special flattened back legs to help it swim. Its front legs are used to hold on to prey while it eats it. Brown in colour, they are the largest true bugs, growing up to 6 cm (2³/₈ in.). They're nicknamed 'toe-biters', so don't go in the water barefoot! Bizarrely, not all water bugs are keen to keep the species well and thriving – there is evidence that the parents may eat their children, holding them in their legs and sucking out their insides.

Do caterpillars sting ?

Butterflies and moths don't sting, but some caterpillars do. However, their sting is not the same as a bee's or a wasp's. Some species have hollow hairs (like tiny quills) covering their bodies, and each hair is connected to a sack full of poison. If the hairs are touched, they release the poison, which can cause anything from an irritating itch to intense pain. So, if you see a hairy caterpillar crawling on you, don't brush it off with your hands, but gently move it with a stick. Remember, though, caterpillars don't set out to attack other creatures – their stinging hairs are used for protection.

FACT BYTES

Eyespots on the wings of butterflies and moths cause enemies to think twice before pouncing. Look at the eyed hawk moth – it's pretty scary!

A male stag beetle defeats a rival.

Why do earwigs have pincers

Despite its fearsome appearance, this insect is really quite harmless ... but it may give a small nip if threatened. As well as being used to stave off the unwanted attention from predators, the earwig also uses the pair of pincers at the end of its body to help it tuck its wings away. It was once thought that earwigs crawled into people's ears, but they would much rather live under stones.

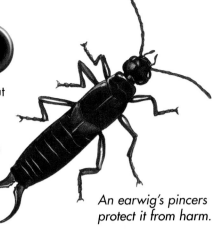

An earwig's pincers protect it from harm.

What is a false scorpion

A false scorpion looks like a scorpion but isn't. This is extremely useful in deterring predators which fear the sting of a true scorpion's tail. The false scorpion has no sting. Can you run backward as fast as you can run forward? The false scorpion can, which is another clever way to avoid being eaten!

How do stag beetles fight each other

If a male stag beetle meets another male stag beetle, he stretches out his antennae to detect vital information. He then tries to look as threatening as he can. If that doesn't work, he'll resort to using his antler-like jaws to wrestle his rival to the ground. If he's lucky, his jaws will puncture the loser's tough armour and leave him dying on his back.

Why are moth wings dusty

If you've ever touched a butterfly or a moth, you've probably found your fingertips covered in what looks like fine dust. This 'dust' covers the wings of these insects and is really made up of minute scales. Some scientists think that the scales make the wings slippery, protecting butterflies and moths from the grasp of predators and enabling them to escape from spiders' webs, but once the scales have been damaged, they don't grow back. So, if you ever have to pick up a butterfly or moth, remember to be very gentle.

A moth's wings are covered in minute scales that look like dust.

NOW YOU SEE ME, NOW YOU DON'T!

Many insects are masters of the art of camouflage. Their colouration may help them to blend in to their surroundings in order to pass unnoticed by predators, or they may use their camouflage to help them catch prey for themselves.

When is a leaf not a leaf ?

When it's a leaf butterfly! This amazing butterfly looks just like a leaf. In addition to its brown leafy colour, it has what look like leaf ribs and fungus spots! You'd have to have excellent eyesight to spot it.

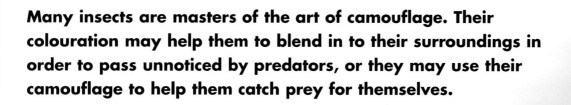

A leaf butterfly

What is a katydid ?

Katydids, with their long antennae and shiny bodies, are strange-looking insects that get their name from the sound they produce, 'ka-ty-did, ka-ty-did-n't'. They have existed for over 300 million years, and their truly amazing capacity for camouflage is a strong reason for this. You are unlikely to see one, as their glossy green bodies blend in with their leafy surroundings, safe from any passing birds or other predators.

Where does the walking stick get its name ?

Just one look at the amazing 'walking stick' insect, with its slow body movements, long body shape and green/brown colour, is enough to prove how it got its name. If a predator approaches, it will remain absolutely motionless to avoid detection until the danger has passed. The stick insect is also known as a phasmid, which comes from the Greek word 'phasma', meaning 'phantom'. This insect's twig-like appearance is such good camouflage, you'd find it very hard to see a stick insect among the leaves of a tree.

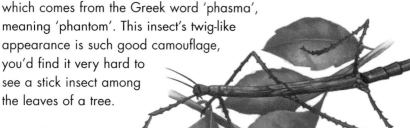

FACT BYTES

Insects that rely on camouflage don't usually run away from predators or take flight, but move slowly and cautiously, staying close to their homes where they blend in best.

Which Malaysian flower is also an insect ?

The beautiful Malaysian orchid mantis lives in the rain forests of southern Asia. It has pointed eyes, petal-like shapes on its legs and is coloured a pretty pale pink – just like the flowers of the plant on which it lives. Not only is this a clever camouflage (and so protection against predators), but it also leads insects to take a closer look, believing they're going to take a drink of nectar from a flower. The mantis grabs these unsuspecting insects – which include butterflies, moths and flies – and gobbles them up.

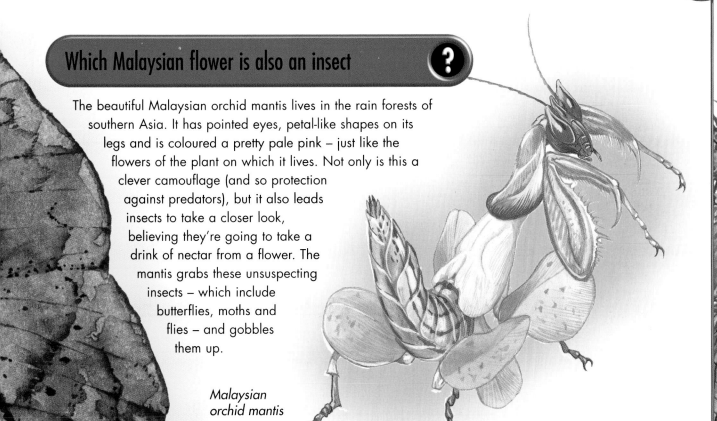

*Malaysian
orchid mantis*

Which crab is a spider ?

Crab spiders are spiders that scuttle sideways like seaside crabs. They use their camouflage as a way to attack prey undetected. When the spider grabs its victim, it pumps poison into the prey's body to paralyse it. The spider then sucks up the victim's body fluids. Crab spiders tend to live in flowers that share the same colour and markings as them.

How do insects ward off predators ?

The cleverly disguised hoverfly bears the same colouring and pattern as a wasp – an effective way of warding off predators. Unlike wasps, it won't bite or sting you so all you need do is remember which is which! The simplest way is to watch it fly. Hoverflies are named after their hovering flight.

A hoverfly

UP, UP, AND AWAY!

The way in which insects have managed to survive for million of years is largely due to the fact that they can fly. Without wings they would find it much harder to escape from predators, to find food or to look for new places to live.

Can insects fly backward ?

Some insects can. Dragonflies can hover like helicopters, fly vertically, stop or suddenly change direction in mid-flight, and also fly backwards. The fastest flier was believed to be a giant prehistoric dragonfly. It was so large that it had to fly as fast as 69 kph (43 mph) to stop it from crashing.

Can insects travel long distance ?

Most insects don't travel long distances, but those that do often use the wind to help them on their way. Some insects have special wings that can help them glide over long distances, and one of these is the African grasshopper. It has broad hind wings, which are perfect for the job.

Giant prehistoric dragonflies

An African grasshopper can glide over long distances.

Why do insects have thin wings ?

Insect wings are thin and light so they don't weigh them down. They have to beat their wings fast in order to warm up their flight muscles so that the wings can get moving. A bit like the way humans do warm-up exercises before sport!

Which insect has the biggest wings ?

The Queen Alexandra birdwing and the atlas moth are really impressive (see page 20), but the hercules moth from Australia comes a close second, with an enormous wingspan of 28 cm (11 in.).

The Australian hercules moth has an enormous wingspan.

Can spiders fly ?

No, they can't – but they do travel vast distances in the air. Small spiders, or young ones which are called spiderlings, can be blown along by the wind across land and sea, which may explain why spiders are found on islands. Some spiderlings have been caught in remotely operated weather stations thousands of metres up in the sky!

FACT BYTES

Bees beat their wings as fast as 180 beats per second – phew!

UP, UP, AND AWAY!

Why do moths fly at the light ?

No one is sure why moths fly towards light. Some experts believe that moths navigate by moonlight, and become confused by artificial lights, such as lightbulbs, car headlights, campfires, etc. Others think that moths are sensitive to certain wavelengths of light, with white lights proving more attractive than yellow.

Moths flying towards the moon

LET'S GET TOGETHER

Most female insects must find a mate of their own kind in order to reproduce. Contrary to what you might think, there are many different rituals of insect courtship, and some of them are quite similar to humans!

Do insects create love signals

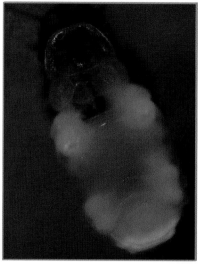

A male firefly flashes to attract a mate.

Male fireflies flash their lights at female fireflies in order to attract a mate. Females are attracted to the male whose light lasts the longest. This is because she reads the light as a signal that he will make a good father. The male has to make sure the female is of the same species before he lands – otherwise he will discover that he's the main course on the menu for her dinner date. Not a very nice end to a romantic evening!

Is mating dangerous

It is to a male praying mantis – the female sees him as just another meal! The male must stealthily creep up on the female and then jump on her to mate. If he's unlucky, she will kill and eat him head first! Bad news for the male, but the female's eggs are fertilised and she enjoys a nutritious meal!

Do insects give presents

Some insects feed on other insects – this can be tricky for an amorous male. To stop himself from being eaten up when they mate, he first presents the female with a special edible love token of another dead insect.

Why does scent matter

The insect world is full of chemical signals called pheromones. Moths have sensitive feather-like antennae that they use to detect long-distance love signals from a mate. Moon moths in India can smell the scent from a distance of over 11 km (6 miles) away. The female emperor moth only comes out at night, so she leaves a strong perfume wafting in the air to help the male to find her.

Which insect sings love songs

Next time you hear a grasshopper chirping, it may mean that love is in the air. It rubs its back legs along its front wing so that it can serenade females.

Dancing butterflies exchange pheromones to confirm they have found the perfect partner.

Do insects like to dance

Butterflies perform special dancing flights to make sure they have found the perfect mate from the same species. Dancing helps to exchange the pheromones that will tell them they have found the right partner. Male scorpions are more brazen – they actually take hold of the female and lead her into a courtship dance!

FACT BYTES

With only one day to live, mate and lay eggs, the aquatic insect called the mayfly is the fastest romancer of the insect world.

LET'S GET TOGETHER

DEADLY CREATURES

Some of the world's deadliest and most dangerous creatures belong to the insect world.

A hawkmoth
caterpillar

Which caterpillar has a deadly disguise ?

This hawkmoth caterpillar looks just like a small snake, which may have a venomous bite. When alarmed or disturbed, it raises its head and inflates its thorax with air to mimic a snake. It even has false 'snake eyes' for good effect. It may have a deadly appearance, but this caterpillar is completely harmless.

A swarm of African honeybees

Does a black widow deserve its reputation ?

The black widow is one of the world's most infamous deadly spiders. Inhabiting the warmer regions of the world, it is especially common in eastern and central parts of America. The venomous female black widow is shiny black, usually with a reddish hourglass shape on the underside of her body. The black widow's venom is fifteen times more toxic than that of a rattlesnake, but because she does not inject much poison human fatalities are thankfully rare. Adult males, on the other hand, are harmless. Like most spiders, the black widow preys on insects. After ensnaring her prey in a web, she makes small punctures in the victim's body and sucks out the liquid contents. The female black widow also has a reputation for killing and eating her male partner, but this is the exception rather than the rule.

Which insect spreads a "sleeping sickness"

The tsetse fly found in Africa likes to feed on animal and human blood. Since the fourteenth century, Africans have been battling with this insect and the fatal 'sleeping sickness' disease it spreads. One bite can transmit a parasite that works its way through the body, and if left untreated, the victim will become extremely drowsy and die a slow and painful death.

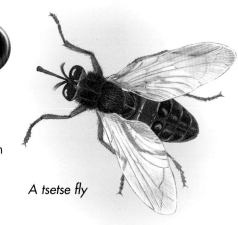

A tsetse fly

Do killer bees really exist

African honeybees or 'killer' bees are a real threat. Found mainly in America, they remain a dangerous and deadly enemy. They are easily annoyed and once angry, they stay that way – sometimes taking it out on their victims for an entire day! Worse still, they target the head and face, so if the victim jumps into the water to escape, the bees will wait for them to come up for air then sting again. Although they are spreading throughout America, they cause fewer deaths than venomous snakes.

FACT BYTES

The South American fire ant is responsible for biting over 25,000 people in the US per year! Once bitten, you will suffer a fiery sting that becomes a blister. Fire ants are very aggressive so it's probably best to steer clear.

What is Africa's deadliest insect

The mosquito! It alone is responsible for the deaths of more people in Africa than any other creature. It carries malaria and other tropical diseases, which it passes on when it bites.

Can an ant sting

The giant tropical bullet ant delivers a nasty sting which gives it its name. Victims have described the severe sting as feeling like a bullet, with the pain lasting for 3–5 hours. Worker bullet ants can be as big as 25 mm (1 in.), so at least you can see them coming!

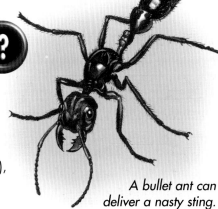

A bullet ant can deliver a nasty sting.

RAINFOREST RARITIES

The biggest rainforest covers an area of 7 million sq km (2.7 million sq miles) around the Amazon River in South America. The climate is perfect for animals, plants and insects because it is always hot and rains every day.

A monarch butterfly

Which rainforest butterfly should be avoided ?

The brightly coloured orange monarch butterfly looks tempting to predators. However, if eaten, the predator will soon regret it. The monarch's poison doesn't kill, but it makes the predator sick – something the predator remembers next time it's passing.

How do rainforest natives use ants ?

Aggressive army ants have large jaws, which they can open wide in order to bite their prey. Rainforest natives noticed this and decided the army ants could help them. Squeezing the ant from behind makes it bite down on a wound, creating a handy stitch and so preventing infection.

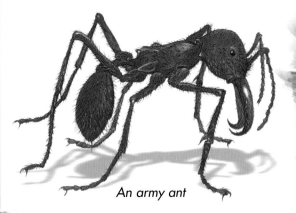

An army ant

Rainforests are home to many colourful insects.

Which rainforest insect tucks itself into bed at night ❓

The morpho butterfly has brilliant blue wings that make it stand out as one of the most beautiful butterflies in the world. In order to ensure sweet dreams and no nightmare predator attacks, the morpho tucks away its brightly coloured wings so that it can blend into the environment. It hangs from trees or the underside of leaves.

A morpho butterfly

Which insect keeps the food chain going ❓

The mainly carnivorous praying mantis can fade into the background and lie in wait for its prey. It is vital to the food chain because it eats all kinds of different insects.

Which ants help to maintain the enviroment ❓

Leaf-cutter ants feed on fungus, which grows inside their nest. The fungus needs freshly cut leaves in order to grow, which the ants collect from the forest. The by-product of this process adds fertiliser to the topsoil, which helps to keep the rainforest plants and trees healthy.

FACT BYTES

A single colony of army ants could contain as many as 700,000 ants, which live off the forest floor. Army ants will have a bite of anything that crosses their path.

Leaf-cutter ants at work.

RAINFOREST RARITIES

WATER BABIES

Next time you're at the riverbank, take a closer look – it's a haven for a world of water insects. Most insects breathe through the holes or gills in the sides of their bodies and would suffocate without any air. Water or 'aquatic' insects are specially adapted to living in water.

What's so special about whirligigs

The whirligig is one of the only water beetles able to swim on the water's surface. It uses its legs like paddles to row its way across the water and can be seen whirling about in groups. Whirligigs have special eyes that can see both above and below the water at the same time.

What is a water tiger

The water tiger is a beetle. Named due to its ferocious nature and enormous appetite, water tigers have extremely powerful jaws. They use these to great effect when disembowelling tadpoles or penetrating the flesh of beetles before devouring them!

What do giant water bugs eat

The giant water bug, or 'fish killer,' is one of the largest aquatic insects, and is a scary underwater predator. It likes to eat small fish, frogs, snails and tadpoles. It can grow up to 7 cm (3 in.) in length. Adult water bugs cannot breathe underwater, so surface regularly for air. They breathe through a specially modified tail which acts like a snorkel.

A giant water bug

Which water insect can walk on water ❓

The aptly named pond skater, or water strider, has a long, narrow body and six spindly legs. It stays afloat thanks to special water-repellent hairs that cover its underside. If you're lucky enough to see one, you can watch how it uses its hind legs as rudders and its middle legs to propel itself across the surface of the water. Its short forelegs help it to catch prey.

A pond skater

FACT BYTES

Whirligigs are also known as 'apple smellers' because they smell fruity when they are picked up!

A dragonfly nymph

Which water insect lives at the bottom of the pond ❓

A dragonfly nymph (a teenage dragonfly) measures anything between 18–49 mm (⅔ in.–2 in.). This clever insect doesn't need to come up for air, as it can breathe by sucking water in, absorbing the oxygen and then squeezing the water out again to jet propel itself through the water.

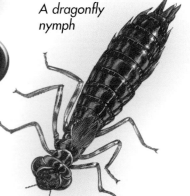

GOING UNDERGROUND

Insects have been living on Earth for so long that they have had plenty of time to adapt to living almost anywhere on, above or underneath the ground. Next time you're out in the garden, think about what tiny creatures might be living right underneath you!

Do insects need to come up for air ?

As they have skeletons on the outside of their bodies, insects breathe in a different way to humans. Spiracles are tiny holes along the sides of an insect's body that act like tiny portholes, enabling the insect to breathe, both above and below the ground.

Insects breathe through tiny holes.

spiracles

What is a mole cricket ?

Mole crickets have a passing resemblance to moles for a very good reason. Their powerful, flat front legs are very good shovels, allowing the cricket to burrow underground, where they eat roots and vegetation with specially adapted shear-like mouthparts.

A mole cricket has powerful shovel like legs.

Which insect helps to turn over the soil ?

There are at least 2,700 different kinds of earthworm. These amazing wriggling creatures tunnel deep into the soil, turning it over and over like a plough. This creates tunnels that supply the soil with air, and allow water to penetrate all of the time. The topsoil and sub soil also mix together, making earthworms nature's help to gardeners.

An earthworm

Which singing insect can live underground for 17 years **?**

Believe it or not some species of cicada can!
Cicadas belong to the hemiptera family,
which means like bugs and aphids; they
have piercing, sucking mouthparts.
Cicada nymphs (not yet grown-up) live
underground on a feast of plant sap –
some for as long as 13 or 17 years!
When it has reached full-size, the
cicada uses its special front legs to
dig its way up to the surface before
climbing on to a tree trunk and
shedding its skin.

Which insects create underground tunnels **?**

Ants are masters of the art of
creating underground nests that are
designed for maximum comfort and
efficiency. Worker ants dig tunnels to
make hallways connecting the
chambers. The queen ant has one
large chamber of her own in which
she can keep her eggs. Busy ant
workers have a number of roles;
caring for the queen or the younger
ants, digging or constructing, or
foraging and defending the nest.

FACT BYTES

During the summer,
ants get busy storing
food in specially
designed underground
larders. In the winter
they help themselves to
their special food stores.

Why is it so hard to pull a worm out of the ground **?**

You may have watched a hungry bird busy tugging at the soil, and it's a
safe bet that there's a tug-of-war going on between the worm and the bird.
The worm has four pairs of hooks called setae, which can stick to soil particles
and make it very hard for the worm to be pulled from its hole!

DESERT BUGS

You might expect the dry and barren landscape of the desert to be too hot for insects to survive. However, many of these amazing desert creatures have adapted to life under the sun.

Which desert bugs rarely drink

Both scorpions and camel spiders are specially adapted to their arid environment and have a very low rate of water loss, taking all the liquid they need from their prey victims. They are nearly all nocturnal, spending their days shaded in burrows or under rocks, reserving their energy to hunt by night.

Which insect is deadly to crops ?

The desert locust. When young, the swarming species of desert locust form groups of around 20,000, and hop about on the sand looking for food. As they grow up and learn to fly they become even more dangerous to crops. Swarms of locusts will fly over the desert eating everything in their path, travelling up to 1,036 sq km (400 sq miles) per day. There could be as many as 80 billion insects capable of destroying 40,000 tonnes of plants in one day!

A desert locust

How else do insects get water to drink

The darkling beetle, which lives in the extremely dry Namib Desert of Africa, gets moisture in a very clever way. Early each morning, it sets off up to the shady side of a dune, where it stands with its head pointing down the slope and its rear up in the air. As the morning mist clears, some of its moisture collects on the ridged back of the beetle until a drop forms. This drop then gently rolls down the length of the beetle towards its mouth, and it takes a drink!

A darkling beetle

Scorpians performing a courtship dance.

A camel spider

What is the camel spider ?

A cross between a spider and a scorpion, and growing up to 15 cm (6 in.) in length, the camel spider can run like the wind, with speeds of up to 16 kph (10 mph). This explains its other name of 'wind scorpion'. Like scorpions, camel spiders hunt at night. They prey on scorpions, lizards, mice and even birds!

Why is the giant desert scorpion covered in hair ?

Living in the desert regions of California and Arizona, the giant desert scorpion can grow up to 15 cm (6 in.). This hairy monster lurks under rocks in the heat of the day, using the brown hairs that cover its body to detect air and ground vibrations.

DESERT BUGS

FACT BYTES

Scorpions and spiders are part of the arachnid family. The Sahara scorpion lives on insects and spiders. It seizes its prey with its pincers before injecting a lethal poison from its tail. Its sting is potent enough to kill an adult human being!

A giant desert scorpion

SWAMP MONSTERS

Swamps provide an excellent environment for aquatic insects such as dragonflies and mosquitoes. Either completely or partially wooded with trees and shrubs, these warm, wet habitats teem with animal, plant and insect life.

What are midges

Midges are small flies that fly around in large swarms near and around water. The larvae perform an extremely useful task, as they feed on bacteria and are very important in the disposal of human waste in sewage plants. They may not look like much, but they help to keep our environment clean and healthy. Some species bite, causing itching and swelling, and they can find their next meal (you!) from up to 200 m away.

Which everglade insect weaves golden silk

The golden orb weaver spider. This beautiful yellow, black and white spider spins silk webs that have a golden sheen to them, high in the hammocks of the everglades. The webs are semi-permanent, trapping insects, bats and even small birds. The spider cleans the web every day to make sure that its trap is kept free from leaf debris and twigs that would give the game away to unsuspecting victims.

A golden orb weaver spider spins silk webs that shimmer in the light.

Which swamp insect has survived from ancient times

The giant dragonfly! This rare survivor of ancient times can be (rarely) spotted in New South Wales, Australia. Its brown and yellow body can be as thick as a human finger, and nine species of this fantastic creature are thought to be still alive, but are endangered.

A giant dragonfly

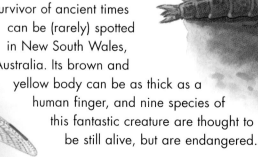

Which beautiful beetle symbolises wealth and power ?

The metallic wood-boring beetle from Ecuador has amazing iridescent wing cases which reflect nearly every colour of the rainbow! The Shaur tribes of the Amazon use this beautiful creature to make decorative ornaments, which they believe symbolise wealth and power.

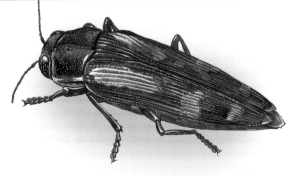

A metallic wood-boring beetle

What is the lifecycle of the bagworm moth ?

At caterpillar stage, the bagworm moth produces a bag made from silk, fragments of leaves, twigs, bark, and sometimes even snail shells which are woven into it. The caterpillar retreats inside the bag, which is visible in the trees, and pupates, eventually turning into a moth. Adult males leave their bag, whereas the female will either leave it briefly to mate, then return, or the male will come to her. The female then lays her eggs in her bag, then dies.

The three lifestages of the bagworm moth

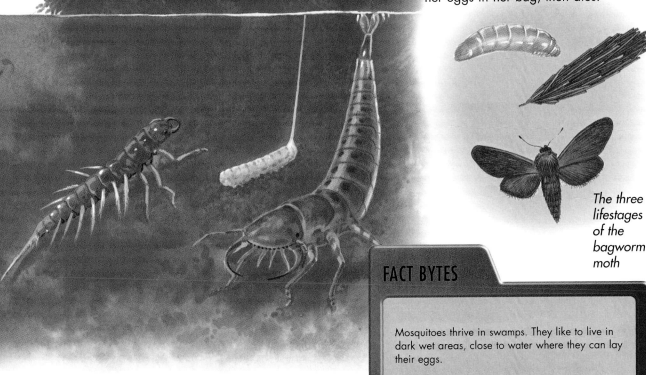

Swamps provide excellent homes for many aquatic insects.

FACT BYTES

Mosquitoes thrive in swamps. They like to live in dark wet areas, close to water where they can lay their eggs.

SWAMP MONSTERS

HOUSE OF HORRORS

So far you may think that most of the insects you've read about are simply too far away to worry about ... well don't forget that some insects are just as happy living in your home as you are!

What is a woodworm ?

Woodworm are the larvae of beetles. Unfortunately, even at this undeveloped, grub-like stage, these larvae have a taste for any type of wood. In the open, they like to eat chunks out of trees, and in the home, they can be found hollowing out table legs and timbers. Examples of woodworm species are the furniture beetle and the deathwatch beetle, who'll appear when the wood is attacked by fungal decay.

How do spiders help humans ?

Spiders are very useful for humans. By controlling the population of pests, such as flys, spiders reduce the damage to commercial crops and protect people from disease-bearing insects. However, many spiders are killed by insecticides and the destruction of their natural environments.

What is a woodlouse ?

Woodlice may look like insects, but are, in fact, crustaceans related to sea creatures, like crabs and lobsters. There are over 3,000 species of woodlouse in the world with around 35–40 of these being found in the UK. Woodlice love damp, dark places and can be found lurking under stones, in old logs and in garden compost heaps. They will also turn up in the dark corners of your house. They have fourteen legs and a segmented outer shell, and some types can roll up into a ball as a means of defence.

Which beetle feeds on oak ?

The deathwatch beetle's alarming name comes from the legend based on the tapping sound that it makes to attract a mate. If an ill person was to hear the deathwatch tapping in the roof timbers, death was said to be imminent. Nowadays, pesticides control this beetle in timber-framed houses, so the threat of the deathwatch is to the oak trees it likes to munch on.

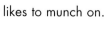

Which insect likes to eat paper ?

Primitive and nocturnal, the wingless silverfish is only 20 mm (¾ in.) long and can often be seen as a silver flash scurrying across a room.

It's a pest in the house because it eats paper, books and wallpaper. Amazingly, the silverfish is more than 400 million years old, so was in existence even before dinosaurs!

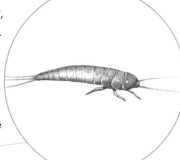

Which insect likes to live anywhere ?

Cockroaches can live almost anywhere, but many prefer warm conditions, so are often found in buildings. They will eat almost anything, including kitchen waste, so often become household pests. They have flat bodies, so are easily able to squeeze into cracks where they can skulk unnoticed.

Can head lice jump and fly ?

No, head lice only crawl. About the size of a sesame seed, these tiny wingless insects live only in the hair on human heads. They hang on tight and puncture the skin with their mouthparts before sucking up some blood to eat.

FACT BYTES

At the end of the summer you might be lucky enough to spy a wasp nest high under the eaves of the roof. All summer long, the wasps will have been busy making their nest bigger and bigger. If you see one, leave it alone! The wasps will die naturally and if you try to move them they won't appreciate being disturbed. You have been warned!

THE EYES HAVE IT

To make up for their size, insects have highly developed senses, which mean they can see and hear things that humans can't. If you are able to look at an insect under the microscope, look into its eyes – they really are incredible!

What are insect eyes like ?

Insects can have two types of eyes: compound eyes and simple eyes, and some have both types. Simple eyes help the insect tell the difference between light and dark. Compound eyes are made up of thousands of lenses, which scientists believe let insects see things in a mosaic kind of picture. Although these eyes, unlike those of humans, are fixed in one place, the lenses allow insects to get a great picture of what's around them, and can detect the slightest movement very easily.

What kind of eyes does a wasp have ?

Like many insects, wasps have simple eyes and compound eyes. A wasp has two compound eyes and three simple eyes so now you know why it comes buzzing straight at you! Wasps, when leaving an area to which they wish to return, act as if they were locating the place, and fly about examining the area before leaving. When they return they are able to find the same exact spot, unless, meanwhile, some landmark has been removed.

How does a caterpillar see its food ?

Caterpillars live among their food so don't need to look far to find the next tasty leaf. They have simple eyes so their eyesight is not very sharp – just good enough to make out light and shade.

A caterpillar

Wasps have both compound and single eyes.

Which insect has the best eyesight

Scientists believe that insects are very short-sighted, as their eyes cannot move in their sockets or focus like ours. Butterflies can see up to 2 m (6 ft) away, whereas a bee can see up to just 50 cm (20 in.). In terms of the ability to detect exactly what's around them, the eyes of a dragonfly are perhaps the most impressive. Its compound eyes allow them to dart around and catch their prey mid-flight without bumping into anything.

A dragonfly has compound eyes.

What can a fly see

Nobody really knows what a fly can see or how far, but scientists do know that each compound eye comprises hundreds of single eye facets. The fly can see even the slightest movement, which makes it extremely difficult for predators to catch and eat it.

Can insects see things we can't

Yes they can! Many insects can see ultraviolet light – the invisible light from the sun that humans and other animals cannot see. Many flowers rely on insects to pollinate them, and the petals of these flowers are often coloured in ultraviolet patterns that we humans can't see. These patterns act like runways, directing the hungry insects straight into the flower's centre, and to their dinner! This in turn pollinates the flower.

THE EYES HAVE IT

FACT BYTES

Young butterflies begin life with simple eyes. As they reach maturity the simple eyes expand, grow and gradually become compound eyes. Compound eyes are excellent at detecting motion.

GLOSSARY

Abdomen
The rear part of the body behind the thorax.

Amber
The hard fossilized resin of extinct trees.

Antennae
A pair of mobile appendages on the heads of insects that often respond to touch and taste but may be specialized for swimming.

Aquatic insect
Lives in, or near, water.

Arachnid
A group of insects including spiders, scorpions, mites, and ticks.

Arthropod
Animals lacking a backbone, such as insects, spiders, and crustaceans.

Bacteria
A large group of typically single cell microrganisms, many of which cause disease.

Camouflage
The means by which animals escape the notice of predators.

Cannibal
An animal that feeds on the flesh of others of its kind.

Carnivorous
Feeds on other animals.

Cephalothorax
A combined head and thorax.

Chrysalis
The pupa of a moth or a butterfly, in a case or cocoon.

Colony
A community of insects living together.

Compound eye
Insect eye consisting of numerous small visual units.

Diapause
A process that makes insects inactive in cold climates.

Digestion
The act or process in living organisms of breaking down food into easily absorbed substances by the action of enzymes.

Disease
Generally an illness or sickness where normal physiological function is impaired.

Egg
The oval or round reproductive body laid by the females of birds, reptiles, fishes, insects, and some other animals.

Exoskeleton
A rigid external skeleton.

Fossilize
To convert or be converted into a fossil.

Glycerol
A chemical produced by insects to act as antifreeze.

Hemiptera
A large order of insects that have piercing, sucking mouthparts.

Hibernate
To pass the winter in a dormant condition with metabolism greatly slowed down.

Honeycomb
A waxy structure, constructed by bees in a hive, that consists of hexagonal cells in which honey is stored, eggs are laid, and larvae develop.

Insect
Any of a class of small air-breathing arthropods having a body divided into head, thorax, and abdomen, three pairs of legs, and (in most species) two pairs of wings.

Iridescent
Showing luminous colours that change from different angles.

Katydid
A green long-horned grasshopper living in the foliage trees of North America.

Larva
An immature free-living form of many animals that develops into a different adult form by metamorphosis.

Lepidoptera
The scale-winged insect family of moths and butterflies.

Mandibles
Jaws of an ant.

Metamorphosis
The rapid transformaion of a larva into an adult that occurs in certain animals, for example the stage between chrysalis and butterfly.

Middle Ages
The period from about 1000 AD to the 15th century.

Moulting
The process of a growing insect shedding its skin.

Navigate
To direct or plot a path.

Nectar
A sugary liquid secreted in flowers.

Nocturnal
Active at night.

Odonata
The predatory insect family of dragon and damselflies.

Ommatidia
The sections that make up a compound eye.

Orthoptera
Long-legged insect family of grasshoppers and crickets.

Paralyze
To cause a part of the body to be insensitive to pain and touch, or to make immobile.

Parasite
An animal or a plant that lives in or on another (the host) from which it obtains nourishment.

Pheromones
Chemicals produced by insects to affect the behavior of others in the same species.

Poison
Any substance that can impare function or otherwise injure the body.

Pollinate
To move pollen for fertilization.

Population
A group of individuals of the same species inhabiting a given area.

Predator
Any carnivorous animal.

Prehistoric
Of, or relating to, a man's development before the written word.

Prey
An animal hunted or captured by another for food.

Primitive
Of, relating to, or resembling an early stage in development.

Proboscis
Sucking mouth tube of moths and butterflies.

Pupa
An insect at the immobile non-feeding stage of development between larva and adult, where many internal changes occur.

Regurgitate
To vomit forth partially digested food.

Rostrum
The long, curved snout of a weevil.

Setae
Stiff bristles on a worm.

Simple eye
The small eye of an insect.

Social
Living, or preferring to live, in a community rather than alone.

Spiracle
An external breathing hole of an insect.

Swarm
A large mass of small animals, especially insects.

Thorax
The part of an insect's body between the head and the abdomen.

Virus
Any of a group of submicroscopic entities capable of replication only within the cells of animals and plants.

Wingspan
The maximum extent of the wings measured from tip to tip.

GLOSSARY

INDEX

Acknowledgements

Key: Top - t; middle - m; bottom - b; left - l; right - r. SPL-Science Photo Library. NPL- Nature PL.

2: Sinclair Stammers/SPL. 3: Martin Gabriel/NPL. 4: John Downer/NPL. 5: James Carmichael/NHPA. 6: Andrew Parkinson/NPL. 9: (t) Corel;(b) Bernard Castelein/NPL. 10-11: Corel. 14-15: Sinclair Stammer/SPL. 17: (t) Sinclair Stammer/SPL;(b) Pascal Goetghluck/SPL. 18: Pete Billingsley/SPL. 20: Biophtos. 22: Corel. 25: Laurie Campbell/NHPA. 27: Photospin. 28: Dietmar Nill/NPL. 29: Geoff Dore/NPL.32-33: Corel. 36: Robert Thompson/NHPA. 38: Anthony Bannister/NHPA. 45: Duncan McEwan/NPL.